Edward Everett Ha

If Jesus came to Boston

Edward Everett Hale

If Jesus came to Boston

ISBN/EAN: 9783743316768

Manufactured in Europe, USA, Canada, Australia, Japa

Cover: Foto ©ninafisch / pixelio.de

Manufactured and distributed by brebook publishing software
(www.brebook.com)

Edward Everett Hale

If Jesus came to Boston

.

If Jesus Came to Boston

By

Edward E. Hale

Edward E. Hale

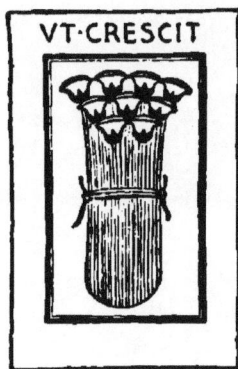

VT·CRESCIT

Boston
Lamson, Wolffe, and Company
6, Beacon Street
1895

PRESS OF
Rockwell and Churchill
BOSTON

PREFACE.

MR. STEAD has written a valuable book, under the striking title, "If Christ came to Chicago." It has excited much comment and much alarm. It has suggested to ill-informed people that Christ's plans have failed badly, and that, as has been well said, "we are all going to hell remarkably fast, — as we are not." We have no wish to abate the force of any one of its warnings. We have no desire to contrast the cities of Boston and Chicago, — which are, indeed, cities curiously alike in many important regards, though not always thought so. But we believe it so important that every student of life should take all points of view, that we are glad to be able to present another picture, as our friend Dr. Primrose happened to see it. He had noted the title of Mr. Stead's sketch, and, to some notes of his week's experience with his unknown friend, we venture to give the title above, "If Jesus came to Boston."

IF JESUS CAME TO BOSTON.

CHAPTER I.

I HAD Mr. Stead's book in my pocket one afternoon when I called on Dr. Primrose. I am used to advising with him, and I get good sense from him, if I let him have his head and do not interrupt him. I found him on the back veranda of his pretty house in South Boston, — high enough, it stands, to overlook the whole bay. A pretty sight, of an October afternoon, when the yachts are all astir, and everything is sunny and the sea is blue.

It is the old Fred. Ingham house, if you remember it. The doctor was at home, from his day's round, and was reading his "*Outlook*." But he threw the paper down, found two chairs for me, one for my body and one for my feet, resumed the two in which he had made himself comfortable, and bade me watch the *Pilgrim* as she beat up the narrow channel against the south-

west wind. I did so. But I told him why I had
come. I took out Mr. Stead's book. I found
he had seen it already.

"Yes," said he, "and they took the Saviour
into very bad places. I could do it here. Hells
and slums and dives, — opium, gambling, adul-
tery, and murder, — I could show it all to him
here, as I could have showed it to him in Jerusalem or Tiberias, or as they can in Chicago now.
But I could show him other things, too, which I
could not have shown him in Jerusalem or Naz-
areth or Bethlehem, — and they could have done
so there."

He spoke earnestly. He turned and looked me
square in the face. He saw he had my attention,
and he went on.

"I should hardly tell you this experience of
mine but that you brought Stead's book. It
was all a little strange to me. But there was no
secret."

He called Ellen, and told her to bring a paper
bag of peaches she would find on the hall table,
and some knives and plates and napkins. When
she had done this, he bade me help myself, and
he began.

CHAPTER II.

DR. PRIMROSE'S STORY.

IT was when I was coming home from England last. We had not a full list, for it was rather early in the year. But I thought I knew every man on board in the first cabin. So I was a little surprised one morning at breakfast, where I was always early, to see a man opposite me whom I had not seen before. We were then within two days of Boston; we had been on the Banks, oh, two or three days. But I bowed to him, and he to me, and fell to talk, — no one else there. The night had been rough, and they were all sick again.

There was, perhaps, the least possible accent in his voice, — or was there? Was it possible that he spoke the English of books, or of the Bible, — and not that of every day? But his face was all alive, his eye told what he was saying before he spoke, and, in spite of you, you said your best to him, as you do when any man tells you the whole, without reserve. We had not talked two minutes before — well, he could have got out of me all he chose. He was ready to tell me all he wanted, and he seemed to know that I should want to do it. We sat long at breakfast, then we went on deck to walk, and — well, I stayed with him all that day. This was perhaps ten o'clock. I had guessed that he was from the east of the Mediterranean, — a Syrian. He had that firm, strong look that you have seen among the Druses. Tall, — six feet high, — as dark as some Italians in complexion, this charming smile I tell you of, and a perfect sympathy as he listened. Strong? Yes, as Julius Cæsar; but affectionate, almost caressing.

He was on a queer errand, which he revealed to me at once, because, as he said, I could help him. He seemed to think that this made it sure I would, — and, indeed, he was right there. Why, if he asked a deck-hand to go down to the steerage with him, the man went at once, as my boy Will there always comes with me, unless I send him away. So, as I say, we walked the deck together, while he told me what brought him to America.

He had a brother over here, he said, " at least I call him my brother," — whom, oddly enough, he had never seen. In fact, before we were done, I came to think that this was only a half-brother, or maybe some far-away cousin who was called a brother, — clearly enough, a sort of an Ishmaelite. This fellow had strayed away, they did not know where at first, till something turned up which showed he was or had been in America; and my friend had come to look him up. I asked about the family, and then he smiled with that friendly smile of his.

Oh, nobody knew how many children there were! Wife? She was a sort of Arab or Edomite of some kind; she must be dead. But he knew certainly of a dozen children, boys and girls both; I think he thought there were thirteen, all told. Anyway, they were lost, and he was bound to find them.

In my stupid way I tried to make him understand that our country is very large, and that people scatter, and that we keep no statistics about such people if we can help it. But he did not attend much to what I said. It was clear that he was used to success, and he meant to succeed. "Legions of people to help, you know," he said, and implied rather gently that he should not give it up before he began. And I, — well, if you knew him you would not wonder, — I "highly determined" that I would not leave him till they were found.

Well, that seemed to be the way right along. I told him, of course, that he must come to my house and stay with me here; and he said he would. But actually, on the pier, after the ship was made fast, waiting on the end of the steerage gangway I saw Miss Burnett, the Young Traveller's Friend, and a girl, whose name I do not know, with the uniform of the Salvation Army. To their surprise and mine, my friend shook hands with them both, and they tried to remember where they had seen him before. I told Miss Burnett that we had these people to look up; and she laughed, and said we had come to the right office this time. She was here, and her friend, for the exact purpose of meeting the steerage-women, as they landed, to see that they got into no scrapes. They had the name of a family from Genoa, about whom the Army people had telegraphed from Italy; and, when all the steerage people had landed, she could go to the office with us and hunt up our baker's dozen.

When they said "hunt them up," my friend looked at me, and intimated that this thing was easier than I had thought. But Eliza Burnett said at once:

"But, Dr. Primrose, why do you wait? Why

not go yourself to Allen street and see if they have not run across them? Then she will telephone to Miss Smith, and they will tell you what they know at headquarters." "Allen street" meant Mrs. Grove's house, where are lodging-rooms of the "Young Traveller's Aid."

And so she took down on her book the name "Ishmael Benagar," which I came to know so well, nodded, and ran into the steerage with her friend, to find the Genoese girl.

I and my companion went our way. I found myself calling him back sometimes, where he undertook to lead; for I did think that if I knew anything, I knew about the North End streets, and I did not suppose he did. He was amused at my persistency in my own plans, and yet, oddly enough, he seemed always to come out right in his. We struck just the right boat without waiting, and brought up, as we were bidden, at Allen street. On a hint of theirs, we went next to the Y. W. C. A. office in Berkeley street. We were shown into the office, — carpet rather worn, long table in the middle, four or five chairs, bookcase with glass doors well stocked. My friend began to look at the books. But he had no time to read before Miss Drinkwater, the chief, came in. It seemed almost as if she had been waiting for us. The upshot of it all was this:

Their index, for years back, showed no Benagar. But every one remembered " that pretty Benaco girl," and every one knew where she was, — with a nice family in Malden, where she took care of the little children. The people were much interested in her, and made of her an older sister in the family. The description tallied so well with my friend's recollection of Benagar's mother, that he took a note of the· Malden home, — sure he should find it, as I noticed, — and determined to go there. Miss Drinkwater meanwhile had called Miss Zilpha Smith, and was talking to her, at the Chardon-street Bureau, through the telephone.

In my dull Western arrogance I fancied that the telephone might surprise him. I did not suppose they had them at Acre or at Petra. But no. He took all such marvels as though they were matters of course. He had to guess from what Miss Drinkwater said what were Miss Smith's replies. And, where he could not guess, Miss Drinkwater interpreted.

" We want a family named Benagar, Syrian people." — " Yes." — " B-e-n-a-g-a-r. If you do not find that, try Benaco, B-e-n-a-c-o." — " Yes." —

"Yes." — "Twelve children besides a girl in Malden." — "Yes." — "No." Then she laughed and turned to us. "They have not found any Benaco but ours; they had her. But they are a bright set there. They think they have them as "Vinegar," — but they have called a visitor to Salutation alley, and they will know in a few minutes."

So we waited, and my friend asked Miss Drinkwater how she fell in with Miriam, the girl he felt sure of. It was a pretty story.

"This Miriam — oh, such a pretty, graceful creature — found herself at a railroad station alone, at ten o'clock. Her father had undertaken to meet her, and was not there."

My friend bowed gravely, as if such were his brother's custom. He said beneath his breath, but so I could hear him, "I go, sir, and he went not." Miss Drinkwater did not observe, and went on with her story.

"If the child had not been frightened," she said, "Mr. Parvis would have taken care of her. Or, if she had met Mrs. Marceline, she would have taken care of her, or, the carriage men are very good, and she might have been safe in five minutes. But she thought she could find her father. He

had written where he lived, and that child, at ten
at night, set out to find her way in Boston.   Where
she went, the recording angel knows.   Where she
came out was at Miss Gardner's house in Berkeley
street, or at the Temporary Home.   They saw she
was all right, and they took her in."

"What do you mean when you say 'all
right'?" said he gravely.

"Oh, I mean she was a stranger, and they took
her in.   That is what they are for."

Then he turned to me, and said he thought we
had better go there on the way to Malden.   But
at this moment the telephone rang.

"Yes." — "Yes." — "No." — "Certainly." —
"Spell it."   And then she turned to us.   "There
is one of the children, Mahalath Vinegar, now at
the Hancock School.   If you get there before
twelve you can see her.   She will take you to her
brother's house.   They know nothing of any
father."

My friend smiled gladly as he heard the name
Mahalath, and said, "That is right, that is right!
I know he would have named one child for her
grandmother."

"But at the office they call them Egyptians.
They thought they were gypsies."

"Well, of course, his mother was an Egyptian."

And then, promising to come again, we left in hot haste for the Hancock-Cushman School. But we did not find it, for all our haste, until the afternoon.

We were crossing Pleasant street, — running, indeed, to take a cab, — when a dark-faced young man, just ahead of us, slipped and fell on the wet pavement. A heavy coal-cart was just turning round, knocked him down, and the wheel jammed his foot horribly. A fez fell from his head as he fell. Quick as light, my companion was at his side, and lifted him to the sidewalk. I followed, as soon as I could, and I saw that they were talking in some tongue unknown to me. I helped to carry him into a shop; but at the moment a policeman touched me and said he had called an ambulance, — and, indeed, before we were fairly in the shop, the ambulance appeared. The men had stretchers with them, so that the wounded man had not even to limp; and when he was comfortable in the wagon, the officer said to my friend:

"I see you can speak with him. Can you go to the hospital?"

And in a moment they were off. I followed, in

a cab I called, and was there almost as soon as
they. I explained who I was, and was led to the
room where the party had arrived just before me,
and where the poor sufferer was already on a bed.
They were carefully taking off his trousers, — his
boots were off already, — and then began the examination of the wound.

The tenderness and skill of the surgeon were
exquisite. The delicacy and silent precision of
the nurses were as perfect. I know I said to my
wife, when I came home, that the whole seemed to
me like a sacrament. In a few minutes the first
examination and dressing were over, the surgeon
looked at his watch, and said, " Dr. Cheever will
be here in an hour ; " and then gently intimated to
me and my friend that we had better go. Bendaoeed bent over his countryman to say a word to
him in Syriac, and then followed me.

"I am not sure," he whispered, " but he has just
the look of his grandfather." And then he begged
me to take him to the chief physician's office, and
I did so. He thanked that gentleman, with Ori-
ental warmth, for the kindness shown to his
countryman. " My brother's son, perhaps," he
said, with feeling ; and he took out two great pieces
of their Eastern money. " Pray take care of him,"

he said. "Take this, and whatever you spend more, when I come again I will repay you."

But the doctor smiled and returned the coins. "Not at all, dear sir. You will have enough other chances to use them. This is what we are for. I am glad you could see what we try to do to every child of God. Your good Samaritan countryman did not live in vain."

And so the Syrian and I started for the Hancock-Cushman School. It is fully two miles from the hospital, you know, so I had a chance to show him some of our customs, good and bad. I remember he was very much touched, at Blackstone square. He stopped to wet his lips at the Appleton fountain. As he offered me the cup of cold water, I took it as a sacrament, and I said to him, "In the name of a disciple." As he walked on he said, "That was good. Did you see the dogs drinking at the lower place, while the horse drank at the trough, and you and I at the running stream above?"

We stopped to see Miss Zilpha Smith at the Bureau of Charities, to see if she had learned anything more of the tribe of Benagar, Benaco, or Vinegar. But she had almost nothing to tell us. This "Vinegar" child was staying with an aunt, as she was called, where there had been an accident, and the Diet Kitchen had provided some special food. That was the chance by which this name was registered.

My friend asked about the registry, and Miss Smith showed him the outside of it, — she would not let any outsider see the contents. An enormous case of cards, which had the histories of the people who had been in need, for fourteen years. But, as she said, if the Benagars had not come to need, they would not be recorded there. Why did he think they had come to need?

This waked me up, of course. I had gone off at half-cock in supposing that they had. But he had misled me; and even now it was quite clear to me that because his kinsman had come to need everywhere else, he had, naturally, taken it for granted that he would here. But there I took up my parable. I said that thousands on thousands of people landed here every year, and with tens of thousands of children, who never came to need. I told him of that New Hampshire farmer who said to me that Cooke could have a fine cornfield, because Cooke had so many children; and I said that the country meant to take care of everybody who came, and did take care of most of them without their coming near any public authorities.

"I thought you understood," said I, "that this is only the margin which we are handling here." He intimated again that Benagar would be sure to be in the margin, if there were any. But I was not so sure. I told him, however, that while we were there, we would see what did happen to the margin, and we went downstairs to Mr. Pettee's office. He is the secretary to the Overseers of the Poor.

I told Mr. Bendaoeed that it would not do to leave the matter to chance, and that this was therefore a separate department, with almost omnipotent authority, which had oversight of people who came to need. Nobody is to starve while the Commonwealth has a penny left. I introduced him to Mr. Pettee, and he to one of the gentlemen who had the oversight of separate districts. This gentleman took us downstairs, that we might see with our own eyes the distribution of food. A tall, thin woman, meanly dressed, met us, with a bag of oatmeal under her arm, and a codfish held by the tail in one hand. A little girl of thirteen or fourteen passed me, and I asked her to show us what she had, which was an order for coal on the coal-dealer in her district. The place had the aspect of a back room in a country store, with bags of oatmeal of different sizes tied up ready for immediate delivery on the orders from upstairs. The visitor who was with us explained that it is wholly impossible to give money to any one in need, unless he fall within the line of certain pensioners, of whose characters the authorities are assured. It might go for whiskey. The city prefers to give the food itself, which is to go into the mouth of the hungry.

Then I took my friend up to the Provident Association, who make the largest distribution of clothing to those who are in need. But my real object was, that at the " Industrial Aid" I might see if any Vinegar or Benaco or Benagar had applied there that winter.

So we looked in at a room where perhaps a dozen boys were sitting, waiting to be employed, and ten or twelve men, — and I introduced my friend to Mr. Peterson. But he was quite sure that he had neither of the three names on his list, and they did not appear upon the various indexes.

As we went out from the building, my companion said that he observed that the gentleman who had gone downstairs with us, and his companion, spoke as if one or the other of them knew all these people. I said it was so, — that the system was such that all these people came, after it had been made sure that they would not sell the food given them to other persons, and that they had no means of earning it by the sweat of their brow. He seemed to understand all this in advance; but he said:

" But what would come to one of those poor people who landed with us, for instance; suppose that in the first hour he lost his purse or his scrip, — suppose that he found himself hungry at one o'clock, where would he be? "

I said I was glad he asked me the question just there; and then I took him up the steps of the building which we were passing, and rang the door-bell. The attendant knew me, for I have had more than one occasion to take a stranger there, and admitted us at once. I said, " Here is a gentleman from the East who wants to see what sort of chowder you make." And the attendant laughed and took me into the dining-room.

At the table there were seated one or two men, and at another table in the next room three or four women. I told him that these were exactly such people as he had described. They were people astray in Boston, who had nothing to eat as noon

came, and they had reported themselves to the
first policeman whom they saw. This policeman
had passed them to the next, and he to the next;
or, if it were far away, he had paid the fare of one
or another in a street car, that he might come to
this central dining-place.

"Here," I said, "you see the fare is not very
attractive, but it answers."

This particular day it happened to be fish chowder, and the men evidently ate it with good appe-
tite. I told my friend that I wished he could
taste it; but it was not for him and for me, and
that I never permitted myself to pass the rule of
the place by partaking of the food which it was
the duty of the city to provide for those that were
in need. Still, looking at my watch, and finding
that we were not quite at two o'clock, I made him
go upstairs with me, that he might see the babies.
In this room were five or six children, not dressed
very sumptuously, but in neat cribs, with clean
sheets, and their mothers sitting by them, knitting,
gossiping, and watching the little ones. These
were the stray children who, with their mothers,
had gone adrift exactly as he thought it might be
possible. There were homes here and homes there,
where they could be received; but it would not do

for them to be sitting upon door-steps while they were waiting for those homes, and accordingly the city had provided this resting-place where perhaps they might be three or four days, until the proper letter should come and the proper arrangement be made which should place mother and baby anew in a home.

He played a little with one or two of the babies, all of whom took to him on the moment. He talked with the mothers and then with Mrs. Crockett. No, she had not kept any record for a long time of the number of people she sent away. The ladies downstairs, of the Industrial Aid, had found homes in the last year for nearly three hundred of these poor women. The truth was that these women were most of them poor creatures broken down with drink, or with worse devils, if there are worse. But there are country towns where no drink can be got, and a little group of ladies, and Mrs. Crockett herself, make it their business to correspond with the people in these country towns. Precisely because these poor women are inefficient and cannot bear temptation, the people in the country can have them, and take them into homes where there will not be temptation. As I said to him, — and I noticed his eye flashed, — " Lead us not into temptation " is a good prayer. So is it that, back in New England somewhere, five hundred people in a year take five hundred of these broken-down women into their homes, sometimes with their babies, and give them the new chance which they do not refuse. Why, they told us of a woman who had been to the House of Correction ten times, whom a New Hampshire postmaster — not yet canonized, because this did not happen three hundred years ago — had taken care of, and who is now living a decent life. His face had its most heavenly look when I told him this, and he said, " I had rather take care of that sheep in the mountains than of any ninety and nine that never went astray." So we bade Mrs. Crockett good-by, and he gave her his Syrian blessing as he went downstairs.

As we went down the street, I said, " You see this is margin of the margins. It does not do to feel that anybody can starve, or even that anybody can be hungry. This is the provision for those who are on the very edge."

CHAPTER III.

I WAS glad we were on foot, because he saw the
more foreign ways of Hanover street and Salem
street better than if we had been in a car. I
pointed out to him the Hebrew signs, but found
they had caught his eye. In truth, after we entered
Salem street, there were more signs in his own language than in mine. He stopped once or twice,
and shook hands with one or another person whom
he recognized as of Hebrew origin, and at once
they would drop into speaking in the dialect which
I was coming to know, which I fancy was some
form of modern Syriac or Hebrew. So we turned
into Parmenter street. I rang the wrong bell by
mistake at first, but was directed there to the
larger of two school-houses, where I sent in my
card, with his name upon it also; and in a moment
we were in the office of Mr. Dutton.

I told Mr. Dutton our errand, and at the first he
looked doubtful. He had not yet, perhaps, at
his tongue's end the names of all the twenty-one
hundred of his charges. He had received two

hundred and fifty girls within a few weeks, but he was utterly cordial and ready to tell and to show everything that he had. " The best way," he said, " will be to go into the school-rooms, and there we can inquire for your little girl; " and he asked how old she was.

This was just what her kinsman did not know, knowing nothing about her but her name. Whether Mahalath Vinegar would prove to be Mahalath Benagar remained to be seen.

In the first room into which we went, a young lady, who was the teacher, welcomed us with charming hospitality; and on the instant my friend said, " No matter what we came for. Let us see what you are doing in your school." I knew that he was interested in all of them just as much as in the one who was conventionally called his relative. The teacher explained to us that not one of these fifty children could speak the English language, not one of 'them was of the blood of the people who settled Massachusetts or who built up the original Boston. More than half of them, she told him, were Hebrews; the remainder were Christian Germans, were Italians, or Portuguese, or perhaps from the east of Europe. Then I asked if they had no Syrians or Arabs or

Egyptians; and she said not in her room, she was sure. But notwithstanding this answer, he was interested, and he remained.

The exercises which we saw were wholly for the learning how to speak English. She told us that while none of them could speak English now, before next June they all would have learned to write English intelligently, to speak it enough for practical purposes, and to read the English of simple books with a good understanding. I do not suppose they would understand a translation from Schopenhauer, and possibly they might not understand an argument for free trade; but for the regular work of daily life they will be able, next June, to read English sufficiently well. Eagerly I asked how this was done. She called up a nice-looking girl, perhaps ten years old, and showed to her a large box filled with every sort of thing. The child picked over it gravely, and then by a string lifted a little basket, and said, with very clear articulation, "This is a basket." The next child would say, "This is a bell;" the next child would choose a box and say, "This is a box." If the articulation were not well-nigh perfect, the teacher would correct, and the child would repeat, until she spoke it distinctly. One

little Italian child had stopped in Paris for a year
on their emigration, and at some French school
had been taught to read English with a sufficiently
correct pronunciation. The only reading which
we witnessed in our visit was the reading of these
English words, quite well pronounced, by a child
who did not know the meaning of the words she
read.

What was pretty about it all was the eager interest of the children. They were clean, their
clothes were clean, and they were alive with interest in what was said and done. When we shall
see fifty boys as much interested in learning Latin
as these children were in learning English, it will
not take boys or men seven years to study the
Latin language, and then find out that they cannot
speak it intelligibly.

We went from room to room, and at last, in a
room where the girls had been two or three years,
this tall, brown, large-eyed, Arab-looking Mahalath.
appeared. She was called to speak with her kinsman, and he fairly started at the sight of her.
Then they went on one side, that she might tell
him her story, and it was clear to me that he had
come to a clew in his labyrinth.

The teacher asked if he would like to take her

away; but he said no, — that she was happy and well with her countrymen where she was staying. He had written down the number of their home, and he would see them there. Meanwhile he would not keep her longer from the work of the school; — and so we came away.

He stopped Mr. Dutton while he could thank him for the time which he had given us, and then, in the same courteous way in which he had spoken to Dr. Rowe at the hospital, asked if he might not be permitted to leave some money in his hands for the good of the poor children or those who were most destitute. But, like the doctor, Mr. Dutton told him that he must keep his money for those who needed it. We explained to him that this was simply the business of a Christian State, — that we were trying to give to these children the best we could give, in training them to be of use in life. We said that we were doing it for each and for all; we would not even leave the parents to say whether these children should or should not be trained in this way. We obliged them to see to the training, in one form or another. If they had no better place for them, we compelled the children to come into this school, and, as he saw, they seemed happy while they were there, and he would find that they came readily and promptly from day to day.

"Our business is," I said, as we came out into Parmenter street, " to open the eyes of the blind and the ears of the deaf, to make the lame walk, and, in a word, as your Master and mine said, to preach glad tidings to the poor in such way that they can understand it. Nineteen centuries would have been worth very little if we had not made some advance in welcoming the stranger, in feeding the hungry, in clothing the naked, and in caring for the prisoner."

He half heard me, he did not interrupt me, — in fact, it was observable that he never interrupted. But when I had fairly said what I had to say, he said:

"When you say 'prisoner,' I cannot help thinking of my poor kinsman. You see, all you have told me is about children and women. Now, where is he all this time?" He said he was willing to confess to me that this Benagar was but a reckless fellow. He had a passion for gambling, and in their own home he wasted all his half of their father's patrimony in what his brother called "riotous living." "Now," said he, "I wish I did not think that he were in some gambling hell, as I believe you say, at this moment." And he asked me if there were any way in which we could see " one of those dens." " Dens" was a word he spoke almost bitterly.

To tell you the truth, said Dr. Primrose, he had me on new ground here. But, as I said, whatever that man asked me to do, I did. I did not say no to him once when he made any appeal to me, in the days when we were together. And while he made his visit to Salutation alley and to Malden, I made the preparation for our visit to a first-class " hell." He said that Benagar would be in the best place in Boston or the worst, and I did as I am apt to do, — I struck high.

Oh, no, it never occurred to me that I had no business there. I wanted to seek and save what was lost, as Bendaoeed had said he wanted to. So I went round to the club, and, in a little, one of my younger friends came in, and I told him I wanted a card of introduction to the gambling-house in Boston where a gentleman from the Levant would be most apt to be found. He laughed very heartily, that I should be the man to ask such a favor; he called one of my friends, and gave me away at once. But they both honored me by saying that they knew I could be trusted.

One of them gave me his card, and then went to the telephone, called Buddy, the keeper of the house, and told him that at sharp 10.30 two friends of his would call, and that he was responsible for them.   Then he gave me the number of the house, and the street, and went to play billiards.

CHAPTER IV.

MY friend Bendaoeed met me at the reading-room of the Boston Public Library. Here I was glad to see that he had a few minutes to see the evening entertainment that a Christian city provides for the dirtiest, meanest, and poorest of its people, — white, black, or red, — if they will choose to come in. Hundreds of men and women were reading quietly there, from the best and most costly books in the world, if they had chosen to ask for them, or from newspapers and magazines of their own country, whatever that was. I explained to him that we must not loiter, that I had promised to be exactly on time. And, by the way, I had noticed before this time, that he always was.

We went in at the front of the gambling-house without ringing, but once within, I pressed an electric knob, as I had been bidden. Instantly a flash-light from upstairs dazzled us both. Somebody inspected us. In a moment a boy with buttons came down, and asked my name. I gave him my card and that of the gentleman who introduced me, and we went upstairs. I noticed, as we passed two doors, that both of them were well guarded by men. But, once in the large parlor itself, there was nothing but luxury.

It was a large club-room, taking the whole of that floor of the house. There were twenty or thirty young men about, — one or two I recognized. I had seen them at Cambridge, or at their fathers' dining-tables. My companion explained to my ignorance that the larger table was a roulette-table, the smaller one a faro-table. In one corner was a dining-table, elegantly served with wines, other liquors, and whatever one might like to eat, with two or three black waiters. Comfortable chairs, and an easy lounge or two, were ready for people not playing at the moment. There were a few sporting newspapers, the New York papers of the day, and in one corner a desk where, as we entered, I happened to see a young fellow cashing a check. He took a handful of bills, and some chips, to use at the moment on the tables.

Bendaoeed looked not so much at the roulette wheel, for which he cared no more than he had cared for the telephone. He seemed to care for no thing, — only for man. A waiter who saw that we were strangers offered me some oysters as we looked round. Bendaoeed refused them, and I could see that he was watching a group of the older men at the faro-table. He bent over and whispered to me :

"That tall man, with black hair, — he is pointing across the table."

But at that moment we heard a tremendous crash on the door below. One, two heavy strokes, as of the head of an axe. A man who, I afterward heard, was Buddy himself, sprang from behind the desk.

"My God! how could this have happened?"

He meant that he supposed he was under police protection. He had bribed some under-officials.

Instantly the lights were turned down, the windows were flung up, and I saw the man next me throw some chips out of the window. The man at the entrance slid a heavy bar into place, so that it should hold the door. The inmates, all as I thought, excepting me and the man at the door and my companion, rushed upstairs to the next floor. "Bang! bang!" we could hear the axes below. And before the rush upstairs of the officers, some one — not I — had pushed up the bar which held us in, so that they entered easily. They put handcuffs on me, on my friend, and the black waiter.   Some one found the gas-key and lighted the room.   The officers ran up to the roof, to meet one and another prisoner; for the roof had been guarded first, and was held by a party of the police.   Then there was careful handcuffing of a party of more than twenty, and we were all marched to the station.   I expressed to my Eastern friend my regret and dismay.   But he said, very simply, that it was no new experience with him, that we could not be of use without running some risk, and that our service to God was worth very little if we could not go before a magistrate now and then.   For his part it was clear that he was more interested in looking up black sheep than in " S'iety " or the haunts of " S'iety."

He reminded me of John Bunyan.

So we spent the night there.   It was a night I shall never forget.   Before two hours were over, all our comrades were bailed out.   It seemed it was a part of the business of Buddy to provide bail for them that they should appear in court the next morning, and a bail commissioner was in readiness.   I told my friend that I supposed I could wake up some friend and have him come and bail us out; but he said he had much rather

spend the night where he was.   And when I saw
how he spent it, I did not wonder.

There was a separate room for the poor drunken
women who had been brought in, and others, old
and young, of their sex.   There was a nice moth-
erly woman who had the oversight of them, and
he went in and talked to them so kindly that I
believe that those who were sober enough to hear
him were other people afterward.   If there is
casting out of seven devils nowadays, he certainly
did it that night with them.   As for our young
college friends, who sat round us waiting for the
bail man to come, it was wonderful to see how he
got on with them, and I cannot think that many
of those fellows were found in gambling hells
again.

By two o'clock everybody was bailed who
wanted to be bailed; and then he and I slept in
bunks, comfortably enough, till morning.   In the
morning, after we had had the fare of prisoners,
we, and a lot of other people who had been drinking or breaking heads the night before, were put
into carts and carried to the Municipal Court.

I knew the judge perfectly well, and of course
he was surprised to see me there.   But he and I
have met in queer places before.   Gradually the

Harvard fellows began dropping in, looking a good deal ashamed, to say the truth. But before our case came up, we had a chance to see a pretty thing, which interested the Syrian gentleman very much.

It was the retiring, once and again, from the court-room, of the judge with some poor woman and the women's probation officer. We both looked at her with great interest. The balance and steadiness with which she talked with these women, and the evident confidence the judge had in her, could not but affect you. What she was there for was explained to Bendaoeed, and how she could treat one and another of these women without exposing them to the shame of a public prison. The three would come out, and the poor crying prisoner would be made to sit on one side with Miss Todd, till she could dispose of her; and you felt that mercy and justice had met together.

Our turn came. The case was explained. I told the judge why we were there, and that my friend was in search of a countryman of his, for the purpose of taking him away. The judge said aloud that men were judged by the company they kept, but that he would dismiss us both, on our personal recognizance to appear when we were needed. This is a mild way of intimating that we had been in a business which the law did not much approve, but that they did not mean to punish us. The Syrian shook hands with him cordially, said he was delighted to see in practice the way in which judicial affairs were conducted, — and we went on our way.

CHAPTER V.

I MUST not talk in so much detail, and really
the story comes to its sudden end. We found the
brother, so called, of Mahalath, who was in fact only
some distant kinsman, and from him got a clew
to a child at South Boston, for whom he thought
he ought to inquire. I had got a side-clew to the
same child from Miss Zilpha Smith at the Bureau.
By this time I had found out that he did quite as
well without me as he did with me; but even if
he had wanted to go without me I could not go
without him, — so that I undertook to show him
through the intricacies of the South Boston
bridges. This brought us down on the South
Cove, where I took him upstairs, that we might
make a necessary inquiry. I tapped at a door in
the third story of the house, and in an instant it
was opened by a young woman in the Salvation
Army dress. She laughed good-naturedly, and
said, " You see I am at work." That was clear
enough, for she had risen from her knees, and her
pail and scrubbing-brush were beside her. She

had moved her patient into the next room, — the poor people there had made room for her till this back room could be cleaned, — and the "missionary" was showing that she understood her business, by putting the sick woman's room in order.

My friend was so pleased, that I thought for a moment he would go on his knees and finish the job. But she would not let him do that. She said, as if she knew him better than I did, "Oh, you have more important work to do, and I am nearly done here;" and then she asked me what she could do for me. We got the address in a minute, and went downstairs; and as we went, he said something about those people who did their duty themselves, instead of commissioning other people to appoint other people to suggest the names of other people who should select other people to do the duty. All this he said as if this hand-to-hand business met his approval in a special way.

I will not say that he could have got to South Boston without me. In the present state of the bridges, it is a science to go to South Boston. But in a little we were ringing at the door-bell of the house I remembered as the Home for Imbeciles, — to be told, what I knew perfectly well, only I had forgotten it, that the Home had been removed to Waltham six years before! He laughed heartily at me, and bade me observe that this was what happened when he trusted himself to my care; and I had to confess that, though I live here within a mile of them, I had taken for granted their administration so entirely that I had not been near them since that time.

So this time we did not go on foot. I called a cab just in time to catch the Albany train; we caught an electric at West Newton on the moment; and one or two inquiries brought us to the door at Waltham.

I cannot go to that Home without crying my eyes out, —and I am forty years older than I was when I went there first. Bendaoeed did not find the particular child he came for, but he found a dozen boys and girls who thronged round him with an eager, confiding air, — well, I have hardly seen it ever on other faces than on those of the feeble-minded. They seem to value kindness so much, and they seem to know that you want to be kind to them. And he, — it seemed as if he could not tear himself away. It seemed as if he had come to seek and to save that which was lost, and as if he had met his opportunity. It was only because he had promised to be at another place at another hour that he left these poor children.

Before the Fitchburg train came along, we had a chance, by a late lunch, to make good the Spartan severity of our breakfast; and then by five o'clock we were in town.

I do not know how many clews he had on his book. In fact, he never seemed to look at his book after he had put the entries down. It seemed as if any chance to help anybody was burned in on his mind, so that he did not need to refresh his memory. But for me, I had one thread of which I had made a note, which I wanted to follow out. So I made him take an electric, and we came to the school-room in Cottage street.

But it was no school-room which we found there. Here were, in two large rooms, groups of children, of all ages, from five years old, well, perhaps to fifteen. I told him that I called it "a children's club," and he was very much amused and very much interested. The boys and girls were all reading, quite as a lot of loafing gentlemen might be reading at the Union Club or the Somerset, — except that none of them were smoking. The school-room had been cleared out, had been aired, the tables had been put in order, and then Miss

Wiltse had come round and unlocked her libraries, and these little witches had come thronging in because these rooms were so comfortable and pretty, and because Miss Wiltse made them so completely at home. She knew what book every child had the day before, or she picked out a new one. She went round, explaining the pictures to this child, talking to another about butterflies or birds, making a third remember about her passage from Europe; and, in a word, petting those children, playing with them, and teaching them, exactly as an older sister might do. I tried to explain that the children would have no such experience at home, — that Miss Wiltse was trying, indeed, to give them a better chance than they would have had at home, without taking them away from the natural affection of father and mother. It was clear enough that the children liked to come. When the clock struck six they went away kissing their friend, and with real grief. She explained to us that the rooms would be aired and cleared and provided with books for the older children, and that after an hour had been given for supper a like session would be renewed for them until nine o'clock. "It is so much better than if they were in the streets," she said, — to which he assented, and I am sure I did.

When we came out on Tremont street, to my surprise he did not come over here with me. He only said, " Do not keep the house open. If I am not with you at nine, you will not see me before morning." And I came home to explain to my wife why she had not seen me for thirty-six hours.

Just before nine, the bell rang, and a telegraph-boy brought a despatch. I was afraid Bendaoeed had come to grief again, he seemed so reckless. But the despatch said :

" *I have gone to Chicago. I find I have other sheep there. What you in Boston have been doing to the least of these my brethren and my sisters, you have done it unto me. B.*"

And I never saw him again.

www.ingramcontent.com/pod-product-compliance
Lightning Source LLC
Chambersburg PA
CBHW032133080426
42733CB00008B/1053